Easy Object Lessons

Charles C. Ryrie

MOODY PRESS
CHICAGO

IMPORTANT SUGGESTIONS

FOR THE USE OF THESE OBJECT LESSONS

Object lessons are a scriptural means of teaching the truth of God (I Cor. 10:11; Eph. 5:22-32). Scriptural object lessons are based on objects which are easily procured (Matt. 6:28; 18:1-10). Such simple lessons are the most effective (Matt. 5:14-16; Rom. 9:19-21).

Effectiveness and ease are the principles which have guided the writing of this group of object lessons. Objects should be easy to obtain so that preparation time is spent studying, not shopping. Objects should be simple so as not to detract from the truth; for truth, not trick, is the goal of teaching. Commonplace objects will help the child remember truth better; for if he sees the object at home or in school, he is likely to remember the truth connected with it.

These object lessons are not complete; they are not intended to be. After reading one the teacher should pray and think about it, adding an idea or changing an emphasis, until, under the express direction of the Holy Spirit, the lesson becomes God's message for that occasion.

In putting out prepared lesson materials, there is danger that the user will think that all the preparation has been done. Not only should these prepared materials be refined for your particular use, but more important than that, there must be individual preparation of heart before they are used.

May the Lord Jesus be pleased to use the truth contained in these simple lessons for the salvation of boys and girls and the building up of His own in the faith.

CHARLES C. RYRIE

Ninth Printing, 1977

IBSN 0-8024-2290-X

Contents

11216

1

Wrong Way—Right Way

OBJECT: A road map.

LESSON: "There is a way which seemeth right unto a man, but the end thereof are the ways of death" (Prov. 14:12).

PRESENTATION: Not long ago I wanted to go on a trip, so I asked a friend which was the best way to get there. He told me the best road. Then I happened to see another friend and I asked him what he thought. He also told me the best road—but it was entirely different from the way the first friend had said.

Finally I did what I should have done at the first. I went to the Automobile Club and asked them how to get there. They simply got out this map and showed me on the map the right road. Well, I went on my trip and sure enough I arrived at my destination by simply following the road they had marked.

It's a simple matter to take this sort of trip, but how can you find the way to heaven? You might ask a friend, and I'm sure you would get some kind of answer. Then you could ask another friend and you would undoubtedly get a different answer. What should you do? Who would be right? You ought to do just as I did about finding earthly directions: go where you can get the right answer. That place is the Bible. Do you know what the Bible says about the way to heaven? Listen to the words of the Lord Jesus Christ, "I am the way . . .: no man cometh unto the Father, but by me" (John 14:6). How can you get to heaven? By trusting the Lord Jesus as Saviour, for He is the way to the Father; and where the Father is, there is heaven.

2

Air

OBJECT: Yourself and the air around you.

LESSON: To present the Lord Jesus Christ as the gift of God.

PRESENTATION: Have you ever stopped to think, boys and girls, that on every side of you is one of the most wonderful things in all of God's universe? It's about the only thing that is free today, and it's something you can't possibly do without. Do you know what I'm talking about? Surely, the air we breathe. But this is not half so wonderful as another gift God has given us, and that gift is His Son, the Lord Jesus Christ, whom God gave to the world many years ago.

I've just decided something. I simply do not like to take anything from anyone, so I'm not going to take God's air. If I can't buy it, I just won't use it. I'll stop breathing. (*Hold your breath for a while.*) Well, maybe I will change my mind after all and take this gift from God. Didn't I look rather foolish holding my breath? And yet there are probably some of you here today who are still refusing to accept the Lord Jesus Christ as your Saviour. When God freely offers eternal life, peace, happiness and heaven, isn't it foolish not to accept them?

But suppose I did want to buy some air. Do you know where I could go? I don't, and I don't know any place where you can buy salvation. God's salvation is not for sale; it is a free gift (Eph. 2:8-9). Either you must receive it as a gift and live, or refuse it and die. What would have happened if I hadn't started to breathe again? Why, of course, eventually I would have died. A human being cannot live without air, and you cannot live eternally without Jesus Christ. If you do not take Him as a gift, then God says you must die.

3

An Invitation

OBJECT: A wedding invitation.

LESSON: To present the way of salvation.

PRESENTATION: Look, I have a letter with me this morning, but I think I'll just put it here on top of the piano and we'll talk about the weather for a while. Of course, I think I recognize the writing on the envelope. *(Walk to the place where you left the letter.)* But I'd rather talk about something else. Maybe I'll look through this hymnbook first. You know, I've had this letter quite a while, but I guess there's no hurry about opening it.

What's the matter? Oh, you want me to open the letter. Well, I guess I might as well. Look at this. It is an invitation to the wedding of a friend of mine. That's kind of him—I think I'll go. Oh, dear, I won't be able to go after all, for the date is past and the wedding is all over. I've missed it. Isn't that a shame?

Boys and girls, do you know what lesson I'm trying to teach you today? It is just this: God has sent us a message which we call the Bible, and in that Bible He has given us an invitation to heaven. But the invitation is only good until Jesus comes and then it will be too late to accept it. In the meantime this invitation to heaven is absolutely free, for God says, "Whosoever will, let him take the water of life freely" (Rev. 22:17). It is offered to everyone in the world and that surely includes you. Someday, however, it will be too late to accept God's invitation; and just as I missed this wedding, you may miss your chance to go to heaven. Why not open your heart right now to the Lord Jesus and tell Him that you believe that He died on the cross for you and that you trust Him to take you to heaven as He promised?

4

Faith

OBJECT: A chair.

LESSON: To illustrate faith and to present the plan of salvation.

PRESENTATION: Today I want to use this chair as the object lesson. You see, I am quite tired and I want to sit down in this chair and rest, but I just don't know whether or not I can trust this chair. It looks like a good chair. The wood appears to be solid and all the joints look tight. I think it would hold me, but I'm still a little bit doubtful. Say, have any of you sat in this chair? Oh, you have. Well, did it hold you? It did. But I still wonder if I can believe you.

Boys and girls, do you see what I'm trying to tell you? The Lord Jesus said, "Come unto me, all ye that labour and are heavy laden, and I will give you rest" (Matt. 11:28), but you will never experience that rest until you come to Him and take Him at His Word. You can look at Him just as I examined this chair and you will see that He is all that He claims to be. Everything He did on earth proves that He is the only Son of God and the only One who can give rest. You can ask any of us who have trusted Christ for rest from the guilt of sin and we will tell you that He does satisfy. But you personally will never know this rest until you trust Him. I'll never get any rest from this chair until I am willing to trust it and sit down. *(Do that now.)* If you want rest from sin then you must be willing to trust the Lord Jesus Christ. Just rest on what He did for you when He died on the cross. He meets every claim. Won't you trust Him right now?

5

News

OBJECT: The front page of a newspaper.

LESSON: Salvation is good news.

PRESENTATION: I thought I'd read the paper to you today. No, not the comic strip page, but the front page. I want you to listen to the news of the day. (*Read several headlines, trying to pick out the bad news of the day.*) These are some of the things that the editors of this paper consider the news of the day. Sometimes, you know, they even put extras out. You probably noticed one thing outstanding about the news I just read—it isn't very pleasant. It's too bad there isn't more good news in the paper, but there seldom is.

It's a good thing, then, that I brought along some good news for you today. I didn't find it in the newspaper—I found it in the Bible. You have often heard us talk about the gospel. Well, that word simply means "good news" (Luke 2:10). The gospel is good news. What does it say? It says that God in heaven loved men so much that He sent His only Son to this earth to die. Why did He have to die? He had to die to pay the penalty for sin, because God had said that death is the penalty of sin. Since God's Son did not have sin Himself, He could pay for the sins of others. And that is exactly what He did, for when He died He paid for your sin and mine. But, you ask, how can I have all this for myself? The Bible says that it is yours for the asking.

Sometimes our newspapers get things mixed up, and once in a great while they print a correction but not often. However, I can tell you without any doubt that the Bible never gets things mixed up. This good news about the Lord Jesus Christ is just as true as God who can never lie. Won't you believe God's good news today?

6

A Paycheck

OBJECT: A paycheck or some money received in payment for some service.

LESSON: To contrast the wages of sin and the gift of God (Rom. 6:23).

PRESENTATION: I wonder how many of you have ever been paid for doing some job. You know that I work and so I brought my check along today to use as our object lesson.

Let me tell you about another paycheck. In my Bible I read, "The wages of sin is death" (Rom. 6:23). My employer pays me in money, but sin pays its wages in death. Since everyone is a sinner, everyone receives this paycheck of death.

If I should go to the bank to cash my check and find that the bank had failed and could not pay, do you know what would happen? Very likely the government would step in and cash my check, for the money in most banks is insured and the insurance would cover the loss. That is exactly what happened in regard to your sins and mine. Jesus Christ stepped in and paid the debt of our sins, not because we couldn't die for our own sins but because He loved us so much. He became our insurance against having to die.

Now instead of death for your sins, you may have complete forgiveness. For in the place of death, the Lord Jesus offers you eternal life. "The wages of sin is death; but the gift of God is eternal life through Jesus Christ our Lord" (Rom. 6:23). I had to work for this check, but you cannot work for salvation. God says that salvation is for "him that worketh not" (Rom. 4:5). Which will you have—the paycheck of death or the free gift of eternal life? If you want eternal life, then let the Lord Jesus who shed His blood for you come into your heart this very moment.

7

Hell

OBJECT: A sulphur candle (or several matches could be substituted).

LESSON: To warn of hell.

PRESENTATION: Some time ago I walked into my brother's new house and looked around. Of course I was curious and naturally opened the first closet door I came to. Well, I got a whiff of the worst smelling stuff I have ever smelled, for my brother was being sure that there were no moths in his closet. I brought some of this stuff along today. I'm going to light it and let you smell it too, but don't get too close or it will burn your noses and throats.

This is burning sulphur. The reason I brought it along today is not that it kills moths but that it is mentioned in the Bible and I don't want you ever to forget it. Boys and girls, this burning sulphur is the brimstone which the Bible says is a part of the torment of those who spend eternity in hell. The Bible describes hell as the lake of fire which burns with brimstone (Rev. 19:20). It wouldn't be pleasant to spend eternity in a place like that, would it?

Isn't it wonderful that God has provided a way so that none of you will have to go to hell. That way is a Person, the Lord Jesus Christ. You see, He came to this earth to die for your sins so that God wouldn't have to send you to hell. Sin is the reason that God is forced to condemn people to the lake of fire burning with brimstone; but if someone would pay for that sin, then God wouldn't have to send anyone there. Someone did pay for your sin, and that Person is Jesus Christ. Won't you tell God right now that you want to receive the Lord Jesus into your heart? Believe that Christ paid the penalty for your sins, and you will never be in danger of hell.

8

The Installment Plan

OBJECT: Something to signify a purchase on the installment plan (either a book of payments or simply an advertisement from the newspaper).

LESSON: God settles fully the account of sin when we believe.

PRESENTATION: Today I am going to use for our object lesson something that has become common in our life. What does this newspaper ad say? It offers to let you buy this television set by paying so much down and so much every week. You understand that this means that when you go to get the set you must pay the first amount and then while you are using it you must pay the rest that you owe in weekly payments. Then, finally, after a long time the set will really belong to you. We call that installment buying.

You know, boys and girls, a lot of people are trying to be saved on the installment plan. They think that they may pay for their sins by offering God a certain amount of good works every week or so. They seem to have the idea that God will erase some of the debt of their sins each time they do something good. I hope none of you has that idea, because if you do you will never be saved.

Do you know how God does settle the debt of sin? Let's see what He says about it Himself. When God saved Abraham He said that Abraham's faith was imputed to him for righteousness (Rom. 4:3). That means that when Abraham believed, his faith was put on his account as payment for his sins. Now you don't know Greek in which the New Testament was originally written, but let me tell you that this statement also means that God settled Abraham's account all at once. There was no installment plan on which Abraham was saved! The instant he believed, God fully and forever settled the debt of sin, and God has been doing the same ever since.

9

The Way to Heaven

OBJECT: A strong board, a piece of string, two chairs.

LESSON: To illustrate security in Christ (II Tim. 1:12).

PRESENTATION: Today we are going to let this chair represent the earth on which we live. Now, the thing we all want is to go to heaven, so we'll let this other chair represent heaven. But, as you can see, there is a gap between the two chairs. That space represents sin, which separates us from our heavenly home. It's a space over which no one in his own strength can pass. Some people try to get across either by overlooking their sins (but the Bible says that all men are sinners) or by their own efforts (but the Bible says that we are not saved by our works).

Wouldn't we be in an awful condition if the Lord Jesus Christ had not come to this world to do something about that gap? You see, when He came He had no sin, and so when He died He could and did pay for your sins and mine. Now there is a way to heaven. We're going to put this board across the chairs to represent Christ, who is the way to heaven (John 14:6).

Now I want to stretch this piece of string between the two chairs and let it illustrate what some people think of Christ. They believe that getting to heaven is like walking a tight rope; they are always wondering if the string will hold them. But God's salvation, boys and girls, is like this strong board—you need never worry whether or not it is going to hold you up. You don't trust in Christ like this *(sit gingerly on the board)*; you can trust Him completely, like this *(put all your weight on it)*. That is the sort of Saviour He is, and that is the kind of salvation He offers you today. Wouldn't you be willing to trust a Saviour like that? If so, then just bow your head and ask Him to come into your heart, and then He has promised to take you to heaven.

10

Eternity

OBJECT: A cup of sand.

LESSON: To emphasize how long eternity is and to present the way of salvation.

PRESENTATION: Do you know what this is? A cup of sand, of course. How many grains of sand do you suppose are in this cup? You could guess, but I wouldn't be able to tell who would be right, for there are far too many for me to count.

I'm going to take just one grain of sand, and I shall give it to you. Suppose you start out and take this grain of sand to New York. Of course, I want you to walk there, and that would take quite a long time, wouldn't it? When you get there, go to the waterfront and leave this grain of sand; and while you're there, pick up another grain and walk back here with it. When you get here I'll put it in another cup and give you another grain out of this cup so that you can do it all over again. I think you can easily understand that this process could go on a long time before you would have taken all this sand to New York.

Do you know what I am trying to illustrate? I'm trying to show you how long eternity is, for the time it would take you to empty this cup one grain at a time is just this long *(snap your fingers)* in eternity. Don't you think, boys and girls, that it is rather important to know where you'll be all during that time? The Bible says that you will spend eternity either in heaven or in hell, and it also tells you how you can be sure it is heaven. The Lord Jesus Christ said that He would give eternal life to anyone who would believe in Him. Wouldn't you like to receive Him into your heart right now and be sure of spending all eternity in heaven?

11

An Important Day

OBJECT: A calendar.

LESSON: "Now is the accepted time; behold, now is the day of salvation" (II Cor. 6:2).

PRESENTATION: This is a very familiar object, isn't it? Do you notice that all the important days on this calendar are marked in red? That is one of the reasons why we have calendars, so that we may know what day it is and what important days are ahead.

But there is one very important day that is not marked on this calendar in the special way that days such as Christmas and Easter are. Do you know what day I'm talking about? I mean today.

Why is today important? It is important because there may never be a tomorrow. It is so easy for us to say that tomorrow we'll do this or that or next week we are planning this or that. But God says that tomorrow may never come for us (James 4:13-15). That is why today is so important.

But there is another special reason why today is important. That is because today is the day of salvation. Perhaps some of you boys and girls who have come today are not sure that you are going to heaven. Well, you can be sure by simply believing that Jesus Christ, God's Son, died on the cross for your sins. If you will open your heart to Him, He will come in and take away all your sin and take you to heaven. But don't put it off until tomorrow or until next week, because today is the day of salvation for you. There is no more important day than today, so won't you make it your day of salvation? Ask the Lord Jesus now to come into your heart and save you.

12

Sinners All

OBJECT: Several children of different sizes.

LESSON: "For there is no difference: for all have sinned, and
come short of the glory of God" (Rom. 3:22b-23).

PRESENTATION: I shall need some of you to help me today.
First, I need a very tall person, then the shortest one in the
room, and finally several of you who are in between. If you will
come to the front I'll use you as the objects.

You all know that the Bible says that all men are sinners,
but I suppose many of you think that as God looks down on the
human family He sees different kinds of sinners. If we let the
ceiling be heaven, then does that mean that this smallest child
is a very bad sinner because he is so far from heaven? Does it
mean that the tallest fellow is much nearer heaven and therefore
not so bad a sinner? Is that the way God looks at the human
race? Of course you understand that we're just letting the different heights represent how good or bad a person is.

If you read only part of the Bible verses I'm illustrating
today you might think that this was true, but God distinctly
says that there is no difference. There aren't good sinners and
bad sinners. Everyone is a bad sinner, and everyone in the
human race is way down on the level of the lowest and no nearer
to God than anyone else. Therefore, everyone needs to be saved
just as badly as everyone else. It doesn't make any difference
if you've come from the nicest home in town or if you are a
bum; all of you need an equal amount of the grace of God to
save you. If you are not saved today, won't you see yourself as
God sees you—a low sinner who needs a Saviour? Then open
your heart to the Lord Jesus and be saved.

13

The World

OBJECT: A bit of dust and a globe or map of the world.

LESSON: To magnify God's love for me.

PRESENTATION: What do you know about the world in which you live? Do you know that it is about twenty-five thousand miles around the earth and that this globe contains nearly two hundred million square miles? I wonder if anyone can guess how much the world weighs. It weighs about six billion billion tons.

But do you know what God says about the size of the world? He says, "Behold, the nations are as a drop of a bucket, and are counted as the small dust of the balance: behold, he taketh up the isles as a very little thing" (Isa. 40:15). All of the nations put together are no more than the fine dust on a pair of very delicate scales. I brought some dust, but of course this dust weighs far more than the fine dust the verse is talking about. God's picture of the world is quite different from ours, isn't it?

This is what I want you to think about. If the world is so small in relation to the whole universe—the sun, all the planets, the stars—why do you suppose God sent His Son, the Lord Jesus Christ, to the earth to live and to die? The Bible answers that question clearly. "For God so loved the world, that he gave his only begotten Son" (John 3:16*a*). It was because He loved me that He sent His Son to die. Why did He love me that much? Simply because He wants me to be with Him in heaven for all eternity. Just think—a little speck like me on this earth that is only dust in God's sight is worth so much that the Son of God came to die in order to take me to heaven!

The rest of John 3:16 tells us how we may be sure of heaven: "Whosoever believeth in him should not perish, but have everlasting life." Is He your Saviour today?

14

My Bankbook

OBJECT: A bankbook (a baggage check may be used).

LESSON: To explain how we know we are saved (Rom. 8:16).

PRESENTATION: Often I am asked an important question: How can I know that I am saved? I want everyone of you here today to know the answer to that question.

I have some money in the bank downtown, and when I first opened the account, the teller at the bank gave me this book. Every time I put some money in or take some money out, the bank records that fact in the book, and I always know exactly how much money is there. The bankbook tells me that I have money in the bank.

When you accepted the Lord Jesus Christ as your personal Saviour, God put within your heart the Holy Spirit. He lives there, and He tells you that you are saved. The Bible says, "The Spirit itself beareth witness with our spirit, that we are the children of God" (Rom. 8:16). That is one way we know that we are saved.

In the back of this bankbook are listed certain things which I can and cannot do. In the same way the Holy Spirit tells Christians how they ought to live. This book entitles me to whatever I have in the bank. In the same way, the Holy Spirit is your guarantee that you are entitled to be an heir of God, which is worth more than all the money in the world. Right now the Holy Spirit guides you, helps you in prayer and aids your understanding of the Bible. That is how you know He lives within. If you are saved He makes His presence known. But if you are not a Christian today, then make sure of it by simply opening your heart to the Lord Jesus Christ and receiving Him as your own Saviour.

15

Another Letter

OBJECT: An unsealed letter ready for mailing.

LESSON: To illustrate the eternal security of the believer (Eph. 4:30).

PRESENTATION: I brought a different letter along today for the object lesson. Last week, you remember, I had one I had just received; today I have one that I am going to send. You see that it isn't even sealed yet. Perhaps you wonder what's in the letter, and if I should leave it here and go out of the room you would perhaps open it and read it. But if I lick and seal it as I am doing now, you cannot read it, for it is against the law for anyone to open this letter but the one to whom it is addressed. If after I mail this I remember something else I want to put in it, I can't even get it back from the post office. They wouldn't let anyone have it but the person to whom it is addressed.

Did you know that when you accepted Christ, God sealed you just as I sealed this letter? The Bible says that every Christian is sealed by the Holy Spirit (Eph. 4:30). Now the Holy Spirit is God Himself, and I don't know anyone in all the world who could break a seal like that. You could break the law and open this letter, but not even Satan can take away the salvation that God has given you. It's also possible that the glue on this letter will not stick tightly and the letter will come open before it is delivered; but it is not possible that the Holy Spirit will leave you or ever die. It could also happen that this letter would not be delivered, but if you are a Christian God guarantees that He will deliver you into His presence some day, for you are sealed until the day of redemption. Isn't that a wonderful salvation?

16

What Death Is

OBJECT: A single cut flower or bouquet of cut flowers.

LESSON: To show that death is separation.

PRESENTATION: What do you think of when you think of death? Perhaps you think that it is the end of everything. In a sense physical death is an end. But death doesn't really mean the end; it means separation. Look at this flower. Beautiful, isn't it? Is it alive or is it dead? Well, you hesitate to say it is dead because it looks so much alive. But really, is it alive? No, for it has been cut off the plant. There is no real life in that flower. If you don't believe me that this flower is actually dead, then just wait a few days and you'll see for yourself that it is.

Did you know, boys and girls, that there is a kind of death that is worse than physical death? It's what we call spiritual death, and it is the separation of a person from God. Everyone who is not a Christian is spiritually dead, for he is separated from God. Now, a lot of spiritually dead people look very nice, just like this flower, but they are just as spiritually dead as they can be. If you don't believe it then just wait a while, and you'll see that they die physically which proves that they were dead spiritually all the time.

Do you know what it is that causes spiritual death? It's sin. Sin is the thing that cuts us off from God and causes us to die spiritually. Have you ever sinned? Then you are dead and cut off from the life which is in Christ. Would you like to do something about that condition? There is something you can do and that is to accept Jesus Christ as your very own Saviour. He died for your sin, and if you will receive Him into your heart, He will come in and take away all your sins so that you may be alive. "He that hath the Son hath life; and he that hath not the Son of God hath not life" (I John 5:12). How about you today? Are you dead or alive?

17

Rejecting

OBJECT: A photograph of yourself or something you have made or drawn.

LESSON: To show what it means to God for a person to reject Christ.

PRESENTATION: I imagine that you boys and girls did not know that once in a while I like to paint pictures. I'm no artist but I do enjoy trying to do a little painting occasionally and I thought that perhaps you would like to see something I had painted. There it is, how do you like it?

I'm glad that you all seem to like it. That makes me feel real good. Even if the painting were not so good, you do the right thing when you tell me that you like it. How do you think I would feel toward you if you told me you didn't like it or if you laughed at it? Then I wouldn't be very happy with you, would I? What do you think I would do if one of you came up here and tried to destroy my painting? Well, I might become quite angry, and you couldn't blame me if I did. What do you suppose my reaction would be if I offered to give one of you my picture and you rejected it? Again I might become angry because you rejected something which I had made myself.

Do you know that God's world which He made is like my painting? He made it in order to show you something about Himself (Rom. 1:19-20). When you look around you or up into the heavens at night you ought to see God in it all; and if you don't, then you are saying that He isn't a very good Artist, and you are rejecting the picture He has given us of Himself. God also made a plan of salvation so that you could go to heaven. How do you think He feels if you reject Jesus Christ who is that way to heaven? Look around and see the Creator everywhere. Then look to His Son in faith and your sins will be taken away. Do not reject Christ. Instead, receive Him today.

18

Ignoring

OBJECT: A dollar bill.

LESSON: To show that ignoring Christ is the same as rejecting Him.

PRESENTATION: Last week we talked about what it means to God to reject His Son as your Saviour. Perhaps some of you, who still have not received Jesus into your hearts, think that you are not really rejecting Him by not receiving Him. But I want to show you that ignoring Christ is the same as rejecting Him.

You have often been told that salvation is a free gift. It is something like offering one of you this dollar bill. Here it is. It's free. All you have to do is to take it. There are lots of ways that you can refuse to take it. You can deliberately get up and walk out of the room and by that action show me beyond any doubt that you do not wish this dollar bill. You can come up here and tell me plainly that you don't want my dollar bill. Both of these actions would be outright rejection of my offer, wouldn't they? But there is another way that you can refuse my gift. You can just sit there and ignore me. You don't have to walk out or say one word to me. All you have to do is nothing and you are refusing my offer. You see, ignoring my gift amounts to the same as rejecting it.

Maybe that's what some of you have been doing about Christ. You are not openly rejecting Him, but you are simply ignoring Him. I said that there are many ways to refuse God's salvation, but there is only one way to get it, and that is to receive the Saviour into your own heart. If you would like to do that today, won't you bow your head now and ask the Lord Jesus to come in and save you? Ignoring Him means rejection; receiving Him means salvation.

19

Power

OBJECT: A glass of water.

LESSON: The gospel is the power of God unto salvation (Rom. 1:16).

PRESENTATION: How many of you have ever seen the ocean? Do you know that nearly three-fourths of the surface of the world is water? Have you ever wondered who keeps all that water in place? God does (Col. 1:17). Look at this glass of water. It doesn't seem very heavy, does it? How many of you think you could hold this glass of water in your hand with your arm stretched straight out from your side for one minute? Yes, I imagine most of you could do that. How many of you could hold the glass for one hour in that position? How about one day? Even a little glass of water would become extremely heavy to you after even one hour. But think of it, God holds all the oceans in their places all the time. That takes real power, doesn't it?

There's something that takes even more power on God's part. It is the work of salvation. For a holy God to take sinners like you and me to heaven required the death of His Son, but now that the price has been paid God is able to save all who believe in Jesus. That's the gospel, the good news that Christ died for your sins. And that gospel, the Bible says, "is the power of God unto salvation to every one that believeth" (Rom. 1:16). When you believe on Jesus as your Saviour from sin, God promises to take you to heaven, and the carrying out of that promise depends on His power. Don't you think you can trust the One who holds all the oceans and all the worlds in place in this universe? That God loved you enough to send His Son. Won't you receive Him today so that you can know the power of God unto salvation?

20

The Cost of Salvation

OBJECT: Your own arm and hand.

LESSON: To compare the work of salvation with that of creation.

PRESENTATION: How much effort do you suppose it took on God's part to create the world? When you think of all the stars, moons, planets, even when you think of the weight of this earth on which we live, you cannot help but imagine that it took a great deal of strength on God's part to create them all and put them in their places and keep them there. But do you know that the Bible says that the heavens, the moon, and the stars were just the work of God's fingers (Ps. 8:3)? In other words, all this wonderful universe around us was the finger play of God's creative power.

What do you imagine is involved on God's part in the saving of a soul? Boys and girls, the Bible solemnly declares that the work of salvation is so tremendous that God, so to speak, has to roll up His sleeves and bare His mighty arm in order to save us (Isa. 53:1). Isn't the comparison astounding? Creation is finger play, but salvation involves God's mighty arm. You see, it is a little thing to almighty God to call into existence an earth or a Mars or a Milky Way, for He simply creates them. But when God wanted to save human beings like you and me He had to give up the dearest thing He had—His only Son, the Lord Jesus. Your sin and mine had to be paid for, and there was no other way to do that except to send the sinless Jesus to die for those sins of ours. That's the only way sin can be paid for so that you and I can be saved, and that payment cost God His Son's death.

The cost to God was everything; the cost to us is nothing, for salvation is a free gift to anyone who simply receives Christ as his personal Saviour. God promises that as many as receive Him, to them He will give the right to be children of God (John 1:12). Will you do that?

21

Kerchoo

OBJECT: A common cold.

LESSON: To illustrate the effects of sin and present the way of salvation.

PRESENTATION: Do you know what happened to me this week? Well, the other night I woke up and my throat was sore and my head was all stopped up. The next day I felt worse. Finally, you can see what a "beautiful" cold I have this morning. So I thought I'd use my cold today as an object lesson to represent sin.

When you have a cold nobody wants to be around you. People are cordial to you as long as you don't get too close to them; but start talking to someone to his face and you'll soon be talking to yourself. Boys and girls, that's exactly what sin does—it separates you from God. God loves you even when you're a sinner, but He simply cannot fellowship with you as long as nothing has been done about your sin.

Furthermore, just as this cold of mine may infect you also, so sin is contagious. If you persist in your sin, the older you get the more you will find yourself under its power. Of course, you will influence others to sin. Be careful, if you don't apply the remedy for sin, you'll soon find yourself really sick and miserable.

I'm "doctoring" my cold. The medicine is working, and I expect to be well very shortly. God has given this world and you a remedy for sin. It's His Son, Jesus Christ, who died at Calvary for your sins. Listen to God's prescription: "Believe on the Lord Jesus Christ, and thou shalt be saved" (Acts 16:31).

Do you want to be saved from your sin today? Then receive the Lord Jesus into your heart. Pills in a bottle don't do any good. You must take them. A Christ who is outside your heart cannot save you. Ask Him to come in and save you from sin.

22

A Stopped Watch

OBJECT: A watch that is stopped.

LESSON: Life doesn't begin until you accept Christ.

PRESENTATION: Look at my watch. It's a beautiful watch, isn't it? Shiny, easy to read, compact—a very nice watch. There's just one thing wrong with it; it's not running. The watch says three minutes to eight, and if I look at it an hour later it will still say three minutes to eight.

Now, this stopped watch is like all unsaved people in the world. They may be very nice people, but there's just one thing wrong. They have not really begun to live because they don't have eternal life. Oh, they're physically alive, but they know nothing about the divine life which God offers to all who will accept His Son as Saviour from sin. And, just like this watch, they will stay in that same condition as long as nothing is done about their sins. You don't really begin to live and make progress until Christ comes into your life.

What good is this watch in this condition? Well, it may be a nice ornament on my wrist, but it certainly is not fulfilling the purpose for which it was made. In the same way, an unsaved person may be a very nice person, but he can never fulfill the purpose for which he was created until he becomes a Christian.

No progress—no purpose; that's an awful condition, isn't it? Well, it's very easy to start a watch—wind it. Look, it's running now. That was easy, but only because an expert watchmaker had assembled all the parts in the right way. On your part, it's very easy to become a Christian. All you must do is believe. He sent the Lord Jesus to die on the cross of Calvary. Now all you have to do is believe that He died for your sins. Then God will give you eternal life. Will you do that right now?

23

All-Seeing

OBJECT: None.

LESSON: To emphasize the fact that God sees and knows everything.

PRESENTATION: My, you all look lovely this morning. Everyone is so neatly dressed. The part of you which I can see is very nice. But, you know, I can only see what's on the outside. God sees everything, doesn't He? And that means that He can see not only your dress but He also sees your heart. Do you remember what the Bible says? "Man looketh on the outward appearance, but the LORD looketh on the heart" (I Sam. 16:7).

God sees everything, everywhere. The Bible says: "For the eyes of the LORD run to and fro throughout the whole earth, to shew himself strong in the behalf of them whose heart is perfect toward him" (II Chron. 16:9). You never do anything, boys and girls, that God doesn't see.

God sees everything; God sees everywhere; and God sees all the time. He sees your actions in the daytime and He sees them just as well at night. *(If possible turn the lights off so that the room is dark.)* Sit very quietly while the lights are off. I want to read you a verse of Scripture. "Neither is there any creature that is not manifest in his sight: but all things are naked and opened unto the eyes of him with whom we have to do" (Heb. 4:13). *(Lights on now.)*

Boys and girls, if you've never faced God and opened your heart to His Son, Jesus Christ, who died for your sins, don't try to run away any longer. Believe on the Lord Jesus Christ today and be saved. If you are a Christian, then remember every day that everything you do is seen by your heavenly Father; so, live in such a way that you won't be ashamed to have Him see what you are doing.

24

The Wind

OBJECT: The wind or your own breath.

LESSON: To illustrate the work of the Holy Spirit and to emphasize the need of responding to His call.

PRESENTATION: How many of you boys and girls have ever seen the wind? Why, some of you say you have. Do you really believe you saw the wind? I don't think you did, and I'll show you what I mean just now. Look, I'm going to blow breath out of my mouth. There, did any of you see that? Now, let me hold a piece of paper in front of my mouth. Did you see my breath that time? No, you just saw the effects of my breath. In the same way, when the wind blows you don't actually see it, you just see what it does.

You know, the Lord Jesus said that the Holy Spirit was like the wind (John 3:8). You cannot see Him, but you certainly can see what He does in the world. Tell me, just because you cannot see my breath or the wind does that mean they are not real? Of course not. Neither is the Holy Spirit unreal because you or I cannot see Him. He is a very real Person who does a very real work in the world.

Have you ever seen a person standing in a cold draft shivering and yet not doing anything about it? That's rather silly, isn't it, especially if there is a warm room he could step into or a warm coat he could put on. Now, boys and girls, the Holy Spirit is in the world and in this very room today to tell you that you need to ask Jesus to come into your heart and save you from all your sins. That's His job today. If you feel the Holy Spirit telling you that you need Jesus today, don't ignore Him. Won't you just bow your head and ask the Lord Jesus to come into your heart and save you from all sin? (Rev. 3:20).

25

Tears

OBJECT: Your eyes.

LESSON: "The blood of Jesus Christ his Son cleanseth us from all sin" (I John 1:7).

PRESENTATION: How many of you washed before you came to church today? How many of you like to wash behind the ears? I guess no boy or girl likes to wash there; but, have you ever stopped to think that there is one place on your body you never wash? Actually, it's a place on the surface, which is not covered by clothes, but you never wash it. Do you know what I'm talking about? I'm thinking of your eyes. It doesn't make any difference how dirty you get, you never have to wash your eyes because tears keep your eyes clean day and night.

Washing illustrates a very important biblical truth about salvation: "The blood of Jesus Christ his Son cleanseth us from all sin" (I John 1:7), and the truth is that the death of the Lord Jesus continues to cleanse you from sin. Notice the tense of the verb in that verse—it's present. You are kept saved because the Lord Jesus keeps on cleansing you from all sin. This doesn't mean that there is blood in heaven, for the blood in that verse means the death of Christ, and the death of Christ once for all on Calvary continues in effect day after day.

Isn't that a wonderful kind of salvation to have? It's a salvation that not only erases the sins of the past but takes care of the sins of today. Just like our tears, the blood of the Lord Jesus works on our behalf whether we do anything about it or not.

26

A Uniform

OBJECT: Part or all of a uniform (like a basketball or baseball outfit).

LESSON: To warn professing Christians.

PRESENTATION: What is this clothing that I have today? Yes, it's a baseball jersey. And here's a baseball cap, and the pants and socks. As a matter of fact, I have a complete uniform here. Now suppose, boys and girls, that I should put on this uniform, as I'm putting the cap on now. You'd really think I was quite an expert baseball player, wouldn't you? I'm probably the greatest pitcher that ever lived, don't you imagine? What's that? Some of you don't act like you believe me. Do you mean to tell me that a uniform doesn't make a player? Well, you're right. Just because I wear a baseball outfit certainly does not guarantee that I can pitch or even play ball at all.

What makes you a Christian? Is it wearing the uniform? That is, are you a Christian because you look like one and even possibly act like one? Of course not, for a Christian is a person who has taken Jesus Christ into his heart as his Saviour and not one who is putting on something on the outside. Being good does not make you a Christian, just as wearing a uniform does not make you a player. God says we are saved by Christ, not by our good works.

Perhaps you would be more convinced that I can play ball if I tell you all about the game. No, you still want to see me in action. In the same way, being able to give all the answers about how to become a Christian does not make you one. You must personally and individually receive the Lord Jesus into your heart so that He can take away all your sins.

How about it? Are you really saved? Or have you just been putting on a front? If Christ is not in your heart, then coming to Sunday school is just like wearing a uniform without being able to play. You may fool others, but you cannot fool God. Are you really saved? If not, or if you are not sure, then right now won't you ask the Lord Jesus to save you from all your sin?

27

The Funnies

OBJECT: The comic page from a daily newspaper.

LESSON: To urge the importance of daily Bible reading.

PRESENTATION: I am sure that I do not have to tell you what I have here today. It's the comic page from the paper. How many of you read the comics every day? I see that most of you do. Now let me ask you another question. How many of you read the Bible every day?

Isn't it strange how busy we can imagine ourselves to be when we are reminded of the importance of reading God's Word daily? At least being busy is the excuse most people give. Let's be honest about this. It only takes five or ten minutes to read a chapter from the Bible, and I am sure that all of us can easily afford to spend at least that much time in God's Word.

I know that most of you spend at least ten minutes reading the paper or listening to the radio or watching television every day. Of course there is nothing wrong with doing these things unless they take so much time that there is none left for reading God's Word and praying to Him. If that happens then you had better turn off the radio or television program earlier in order to have time for Bible reading. I know that when some of you miss one of your favorite comics for even one day that you can hardly wait until you see what happens the next day. Don't you think that God's Word deserves the same daily interest?

Suppose we make this a matter of prayer together right now and ask the Lord to help us make time for His Word every single day. I know the Lord will hear and answer such a prayer if you are willing to pray it. Shall we bow our heads and talk to Him about it?

28

Dark Glasses

OBJECT: A pair of dark glasses.

LESSON: Sin colors spiritual perception.

PRESENTATION: Today we are going to have another object lesson about a pair of glasses. But take a look at this pair. You see that this pair of glasses has colored lenses. What did the regular glasses represent? Yes, the Holy Spirit. What do you suppose this dark pair represents? It represents sin that comes into the life of the Christian and colors his outlook so that he cannot see things as they really are. These are Satan's glasses, which he tries to make you wear.

Let me give you an illustration of how Satan works. You know that God does not want His children to lie. But there are Christian boys and girls who sometimes, when they get into trouble, try to squirm out of it by telling a lie. Only they don't call it a lie. They call it a "white lie." Let me tell you that there is no such thing as a "white lie"—all lies are black. What has happened is this: Satan has put a pair of dark glasses on that boy or girl and he or she doesn't see clearly that the Bible says not to lie (Col. 3:9).

This is a very serious matter, boys and girls, for when sin gets into our lives we are grieving the Holy Spirit, and God tells us not to do that (Eph. 4:30). What about you today? Are you wearing dark glasses that are coloring your ability to understand the Bible? Whatever your dark glasses may be made of—whether temper, or hate, or disobedience, or lying—confess the sin to God right now and He will forgive you. Then you will be able to see clearly again.

29

Balloon or Brick

OBJECT: An inflated balloon and a brick.

LESSON: What kind of Christian are you in a pinch?

PRESENTATION: I'm going to let the two objects today represent two individual Christians. Don't be surprised if one of them acts much like any Christian you know. This Christian over here *(hold up the balloon)* is the sort of person who talks a lot. We sometimes say he is full of hot air. He can tell you that all you have to do to be saved is to believe on the Lord Jesus Christ; he answers all the questions in Sunday school; he talks big before the other boys and girls about how long he has been a Christian. Do you know anyone like that?

Now this other fellow *(hold up the brick)* is a Christian too, but he is just as solid as a rock. Yes, he also talks about the Lord and answers questions in Sunday school, but what he says he backs up with his life. You can really count on him, for just like this brick, he is solid through and through.

But watch—Satan comes along. He puts some temptation in the path of each of these Christians. Perhaps their schoolmates call them sissies when they begin to tell about the Lord Jesus. Has Satan ever done that to you? What kind of a Christian were you in the pinch? Were you a brick Christian *(pinch the brick)*, or a balloon Christian *(pinch the balloon until it bursts)*?

What kind of Christian does the Lord Jesus want you to be in the pinch? Like the brick, of course. But do you know how to be like that? Read your Bible, pray every day to the Lord and, above all, back up everything you say with the way you live. Are you a balloon or a brick Christian?

30

Cleaning Up

OBJECT: Several toilet articles such as those mentioned in the presentation.

LESSON: To emphasize the concern a Christian should have for a clean heart (I John 1:9).

PRESENTATION: I'm sure all of you know what this is. Yes, it's a washcloth, and of course you use it to wash your face—and also your ears when Mother is watching! How many of you washed your face this morning? Now, what is this? Yes, a toothbrush. How many of you brushed your teeth this morning? Here's a comb. I wonder how many of you used one of these today. *(Other items such as a fingernail file, clothes brush and shoe brush may be added to the list, but they should all be items used for cleaning purposes.)*

I know that all of you used one or more of these articles this very day, and I suppose that most of you spent quite a little time cleaning up before you came today. But let me ask you a serious question. How much time did you spend cleaning up on the inside today? You know that the Bible says that "man looketh on the outward appearance, but the LORD looketh on the heart" (I Sam. 16:7). Don't you think, then, that it's much more important that you be clean on the inside?

But how can you do that? Surely none of these objects will clean the heart. Shall I try the toothbrush or the hairbrush? It would be foolish, wouldn't it? But there is something that will clean the heart, and that is the blood of the Lord Jesus Christ. If you are not a Christian this morning, then simply open your heart to Him, and He will come in and cleanse it from all sin. If you are a Christian and there is sin in your life, all you need to do is to confess it—and that same blood will cleanse your heart so that your fellowship with God may be restored.

31

Secure

OBJECT: Your own hand.

LESSON: "No man is able to pluck them out of my Father's hand" (John 10:29).

PRESENTATION: No, I'm not going to fight with any of you today —my clenched fist is the object lesson. Now I want the smallest one here to try to get my hand open. You can't do it, can you, and if I had something valuable in my hand you wouldn't be able to get it, would you?

Do you know how the Bible describes the position of every Christian? Each one who has trusted Christ is seen to be held tightly in the hand of God (John 10:28-29). You see, I didn't choose the smallest person to try to open my fist just because I was afraid someone else might be able to do it, but I did it in order to emphasize the contrast between the strength of the hand of God and the lack of strength in puny, weak man. I know that there are lots of people who could force me to open my hand, but I don't know of anyone who is able to force open the hand of God and attack any Christian who is held securely in it.

Do you know how strong God's hand is? Well, the Bible says that His fingers created all the stars and moon and things we see in the heavens above (Ps. 8:3). Imagine, God did that with His fingers! How strong, then, do you think His hands are? Are they strong enough to hold you secure for all time and eternity? Of course they are.

But there may be someone here today who does not know about such security. Would you like to know how to have it? The Bible says that if you will come to the Lord Jesus Christ and receive Him as your Saviour He will freely give you eternal life.

32

Trapped

OBJECT: A mousetrap.

LESSON: To point out the deceitfulness of sin.

PRESENTATION: I've been having trouble with mice at my house this week, so I thought I'd bring along the mousetrap and use it for our object lesson. This is a fine trap. Look at the fine piece of wood from which it is made. I'm sure that it will help catch my mouse. Look at this fine spring that sets the trap off and kills the mouse. I'm sure that plays an important part in catching the mouse. Look how sturdy the whole thing is. No mouse would walk away with a trap like this one. Look what a clever place there is to put the bait. Surely you'll agree that this is a fine mouse trap.

But what catches the mouse? The wood, or the spring, or the sturdiness? No, the cheese. And, you know, it's such a tiny bit of cheese that I wouldn't even know it was there if I tried to make a sandwich out of it. But when that mouse comes up to the trap all he notices is that bit of cheese and that's all he cares about. Only when it's too late does he realize that the cheese led him to the trap.

Boys and girls, beware that Satan doesn't deceive you into sin by a little bit of his tantalizing cheese. Sin is pleasure (Heb. 11:25), but that moment of pleasure may trap you so that you find yourself in the complete control of sin. Take a good look beyond the bait and realize just how bad sin is and how deceitful it can be. Satan wants to tempt you, but do not underestimate his power, for his traps have attractive bait and they are strong and sturdy. Remember the mousetrap when you go out to play and when you are in school. Don't let anyone tell you that this or that is just a little sin and not very wrong. That's Satan's bait. It is all sin. Don't be trapped.

33

A Grade Book

OBJECT: A teacher's grade book.

LESSON: To demonstrate the principle of the judgment of Christians (I Cor. 3:11-15).

PRESENTATION: I suppose that most of you boys and girls have seen the object I have today, for I brought along my grade book. I don't have to tell you what this is used for, because you all know too well—especially toward the end of the school year.

But do you know that God has a grade book in which is written the name of every person who has received the Lord Jesus as his Saviour? Do you know what He is keeping in His grade book? The Bible tells us that God is keeping a record of all the things that each Christian has done since the day he was saved. (Read I Cor. 3:11-15.) It's clear from what I've just read that only Christians have their names in this book because they are the only ones who have built on the foundation Jesus Christ. Someday when Jesus comes again He will open up this book and see what kind of things you have done since you were saved. For the good works He will give a reward in the form of a crown, but the bad works will be burned. I wonder what kind of a record you are making in your Christian life.

Please do not be confused about this. This has nothing to do with your being saved. God saves you when you trust His Son as your Saviour, but then He requires you to live for Him. This grade book is concerned with your Christian life. Don't forget this grade book, for God who sees everything is surely keeping a grade book of your life.

34

A Love Letter

OBJECT: A letter from a loved one.

LESSON: To encourage the reading of the Scriptures.

PRESENTATION: Do you know what I have here? It's a letter from my father (or mother, wife, etc.). One day this week the postman stopped at my house and left this letter. What do you think I did when he brought it? Do you think I left it lying around on the table unopened? Of course not. I read it as soon as it came. And yet, boys and girls, God has sent you the most wonderful love letter ever written, and many of you have not opened it all week. You know that I'm talking about the Bible, for that is God's love letter to man. Who can give me a verse in the Bible that shows it is a love letter? (John 3:16; 13:34; I John 4:10; Rev. 1:5). Just think—God loves *you,* and He loved you so much that He sent His son, the Lord Jesus Christ, to this earth to die for you in order that you might be with Him forever in heaven. That's the love story of the Bible. How could anyone leave a letter like that unopened?

Do you think I threw my love letter away after I had finished reading it? No, I have read it again and again during the week. Don't you think that would be a good thing to do with God's love letter? If you have a difficult time reading then ask Mother or Dad to read the Bible to you. I don't suppose anyone here has read it completely through, but if you have, you can surely read it again and again and find something new each time. Don't you think God's wonderful Book deserves more time, thought and attention than any love letter you might receive from someone on earth? Will you promise God today that you will begin to read His Book regularly?

35

Promises

OBJECT: Several different pieces of paper money (foreign, play, U.S.).

LESSON: To show that the promises of God are as good as God.

PRESENTATION: Just look at all the money I have today. Do you know what paper money is? It's a promise by the person who printed it to pay a similar amount in coin. Let's read what is printed on the United States dollar: "This certifies that there is on deposit in the treasury of the United States of America one dollar in silver payable to the bearer on demand." Our government is promising to pay you a silver dollar for this piece of paper.

I'm telling you this because I want to remind you of the promises that God has made in His Word. Let's recite some of the promises of God. (Phil. 4:13; 4:19; John 3:16; Matt. 21:22). Now tell me, how good are these promises? They are just as good as God who is behind them. It is possible that some day the United States government might fail, but it is never possible that God will fail. His promises are always good.

Would you like to have this piece of play money? Of course it wouldn't do you much good because it isn't worth anything since there is no one behind it to make it good. How about this foreign bill? It's worth something, but not so much as the United States dollar. But if I offer you this American dollar I'm sure you would take it because you know who stands behind it. What about the promises of God? Will you take them? Isn't it foolish not to take God at His Word when we know He has never failed? If you are not saved today, then won't you believe that the Lord Jesus died for you and that He will save you?

36

Mosquito Bites

OBJECT: Some citronella or insect repellent.

LESSON: To present the preventive power of the Word of God (Ps. 119:11).

PRESENTATION: I know that all of you have been bitten by mosquitoes at some time, and it isn't very pleasant, is it? Well, I've got something here that keeps mosquitoes away—it's called citronella and, best of all, it really works. And yet mosquito bites aren't a bit bad in comparison to something that can and does happen in the life of every Christian. I'm talking about sin in the Christian's life, for even after we are saved we still sin. Wouldn't it be wonderful if there could be some way to keep sin out of our lives? There is a way, for we read in the Bible, "Thy word have I hid in mine heart, that I might not sin against thee." The Bible is God's citronella against sin.

Now boys and girls, wouldn't I be foolish if, knowing that I was camping for instance and having a bottle of citronella, I deliberately left the bottle at home? I'm afraid I would have many bites before morning. Every day you go out into the world of sin. Can you expect your Bible which is at home on the shelf and which hasn't been opened for weeks to protect you from that sin? It just won't work. What does the verse say? "In *my* heart." The citronella has to be on you, and the Word of God has to be in *your heart*—not in your mother's or Sunday school teacher's—if it is going to do any good.

But there is something else that is important too. Do you think the citronella I put on last year will do me any good this year? Of course not; it must be applied again and again. In the same way, you must keep reading and keep memorizing the Bible if it is going to keep you from sin. This is God's preventive for sin. Use it, will you?

37

Labeled

OBJECT: Any label (as from a can of food).

LESSON: The label of the Christian is love (John 13:35).

PRESENTATION: What's this? Yes, a label from a can of corn. Why do we have labels anyway? Why does a manufacturer go to all the trouble and expense to put a label on a can? Of course it's so that we may know what is on the inside. If this label were not on this can I would have to open it to know what is inside.

Did you know that every Christian boy or girl here today is supposed to have a label on? Do you know what it is? Listen to the words of the Lord Jesus: "A new commandment I give unto you, That ye love one another; as I have loved you, that ye also love one another. By this shall all men know that ye are my disciples, if ye have love one to another" (John 13:34-35). The label of the Christian is love. In other words, the world will know that Christ lives in your heart if you have love for other people. Love on the outside shows Christ on the inside. If there is no love then others can't tell whether or not you are a Christian because they can't open you up and look on the inside. All people can do is read the label. Certainly when your temper flares up and you get mad at the least little thing, you're not labeling yourself as a Christian.

If you are not certain if the Lord Jesus is in your heart, then right now be certain by simply asking Him to come in. He has promised that He will (Rev. 3:20), and when He does come in remember that the label He wants you to wear is the label of love.

41

38

Rotten

OBJECT: A piece of rotten fruit.

LESSON: "Know ye not that a little leaven leaveneth the whole lump?" (I Cor. 5:6).

PRESENTATION: I didn't bring a very pleasant looking object this morning. Look, it's an apple that has begun to rot. You know, the other week I got a bushel of these apples; but since I couldn't use them all at once and since it is fairly cool these days, I just left them in the bushel basket. Lo and behold, when I went to get some this week I found that several of them were rotting. Then I discovered why. It was because this one had rotted and all the apples packed around it were also beginning to rot.

Do you know what Bible truth this illustrates? Paul says that a little leaven leaveneth the whole lump. Paul is using a different illustration, but the truth he is telling us is the same— the slightest bit of corruption leads to more corruption. In other words, the little sin in your life may soon lead to something bigger and that may soon spread to others. This rot in this apple started with just a tiny speck, but soon it grew and spread, just as sin—even though it is small when it begins— grows and spreads throughout the whole life. And then the rot spread to the other apples around it, just as your influence, whether good or bad, affects other boys and girls.

Maybe you are using some little word that isn't just right, or maybe you are tempted once in a while to do something you know isn't quite proper. Be careful, because that will soon spread to something bigger. Every time something like that happens, go right to the Lord Jesus and tell Him about it. He promises to forgive you (I John 1:9). Then ask Him to help you not to do or say it again.

39

Faded Flowers

OBJECT: A bouquet of faded flowers.

LESSON: Present your life to God while you are young.

PRESENTATION: Look, boys and girls, I brought a present for you today. See, it's a pretty bouquet of flowers, and I'll be glad to give a flower to anyone who wants one. Maybe you will want to put it in your hair or buttonhole. Would you like a flower?

Why, what's the matter? Doesn't anyone wish to have one of these flowers? Oh, perhaps you think they aren't so pretty because they are wilted? Do you mean that you would rather have a fresh flower? Well, to tell the truth, so would I, and I've only been saying all this in order to illustrate something important to you.

Do you know what is the most important thing you can do after you have taken the Lord Jesus into your heart? The Bible says that it is to give Him your life. You see, men and women and boys and girls are the only instruments through which God can work on earth. He doesn't use angels today or animals to tell others about the Lord Jesus, but He does use human beings. So it is quite natural that He should ask you to give Him the forty or fifty or sixty years of the life that you may have to live.

Do you suppose that God would rather have your life now when you have fifty or so years to give, or do you think He would rather have you wait until you are quite old? Do you think He wants a pretty, fresh flower or a faded one? Of course you know the answer; so right now wouldn't you like to tell the Lord Jesus that He may have all of your life for whatever purpose He wishes? If you will do that you will be giving God the thing He wants most from any child of His. Won't you do it now?

40

The Shadow

OBJECT: Your own shadow. (If possible arrange your position so that your body casts a shadow in the room.)

LESSON: Every Christian has an influence on others.

PRESENTATION: You'll have to excuse me for standing in this peculiar position, but I want you to be able to see the object clearly. It's my shadow. See it? This represents my influence I have as a Christian.

How many of you have a shadow? All of you, of course. There is not a single person no matter how young he is who does not have an influence on others. Do you think I can get away from my shadow? No, everywhere I go in the open my shadow goes with me. Isn't it strange that some Christians think that there are times and places when it does not make any difference how they live, just because they think no one sees them? Don't you realize that everything you do and say affects others? Even here there are some unsaved boys and girls who won't come to Sunday school simply because of the way some of you act around them. What sort of influence is that?

There's another interesting thing about my shadow. Sometimes I'm not even aware that it is there, but it's still there, isn't it? In the same way, even though you may not be aware of influencing others, you can never tell who is watching your Christian life. It is important to live as the Lord Jesus would want you to every moment.

What makes a good strong shadow? Being right out in the bright sun. Do you know what makes a good strong Christian influence? The same thing—only it is spelled differently. It is being right with the S-o-n, and of course I mean your relationship with the Lord Jesus.

41

Confidence

OBJECT: Some kind of transportation ticket and/or a time-table.

LESSON: "Being confident of this very thing, that he which hath begun a good work in you will perform it until the day of Jesus Christ" (Phil. 1:6).

PRESENTATION: Most of you know that soon I'm planning to take a trip on the train, and so I thought we might use my ticket as the object lesson today. I'm planning to go nearly two thousand miles, and that's a long distance. Do you suppose I'll arrive safely? I expect I will, and I'm sure that no one here would be afraid to make such a long journey.

Why is it that I trust the railroad to take me through? For one reason, I know that it has taken others just as far and farther. In spite of rain, snow and other trains, they still manage to arrive safely almost always. When you think of all the things involved, it is really quite remarkable; but we know that the railroad men plan things in great detail and well in advance. Even if you had never been on a train I think you'd go, especially if Mother or Dad said it was all right. Won't you believe that God has planned out your salvation in every detail, and won't you take my word that He will take you to heaven if you will trust Him as your Saviour?

Actually you don't have to take my word for it, because you can go to the Bible where God Himself has written the promises concerning heaven. People will read a timetable and believe that it is true; won't you believe that the Bible is true? The Bible declares that the Lord Jesus will take you all the way to heaven, so won't you trust the Son of God who died and who rose again and who now lives in heaven to take you there, too? If you have never believed in Him, do it now.

42

Weights

OBJECT: A barbell would be ideal; otherwise, any heavy object.

LESSON: Weights of the Christian life (Heb. 12:1).

PRESENTATION: I wonder how many of you have ever run in a race. I wish those of you who have would raise your hands. Now, how many of you are Christians? I see that more of you raised your hands on this question, yet every one of you who says he is a Christian ought to say that he is running in a race. You see, God tells us that the Christian life is a race, for we read in Hebrews 12:1, "Let us run with patience the race that is set before us."

We aren't having a race today, but the next time I run in one I think I shall carry along with me these weights. What is the matter? Don't you think that will help me win the race? Why not? Is there any law or rule against carrying one of these in each hand while running the race? Of course there isn't. Then why not do it? After all it would give me more exercise. Yes, I know as well as you do that anyone who wants to win isn't going to be weighted down with any unnecessary object.

How about this Christian race? Do you suppose that there might possibly be anything like these weights in it? Yes there are, and they are not necessarily things that are wrong or against the rules, but they are things that will keep you from being a winner. Maybe it is some word you say, or some place you have a habit of going, or even some close friend. Whatever it is, the Bible says to lay it aside in order that you may be a winner in the Christian life. Being a winner is worth any sacrifice you could make. Ask the Lord to show you any weights in your life and then lay them aside.

43

Shoes

OBJECT: Several different types of shoes.

LESSON: To show the Christian's responsibility to witness.

PRESENTATION: I almost need a box today to bring all the objects for our lesson. Look what I have here. It's a pair of tennis shoes. What does one use these for? For a special purpose, of course, such as for playing tennis or for some other game. But you surely wouldn't wear them to a formal and fancy dinner party, would you?

Here is a pair of track shoes. You see that they have spikes on them, and of course these spikes are necessary in running a fast race. But you wouldn't wear these around the house, would you? Not only would the spikes be bad for the floors but they would also make walking difficult. *(Other shoes may be substituted or added.)*

Did you know that the Christian has a pair of shoes? His shoes are readiness to tell others about the Lord Jesus, for the Bible says that the Christian's feet are to be "shod with the preparation of the gospel of peace" (Eph. 6:15). I hope that none of you are walking around barefooted, for the Lord wants us to be always ready to tell others about Him. That may mean talking directly to your schoolmates or your parents, and it certainly means always living the kind of life that would let everyone know that you belong to the Lord Jesus. It may mean inviting someone to come with you here next week. When you have shoes on no one sees your feet, do they? In the same way, in the Christian walk no one should see you but only the Lord in your life. And yet I hear so many boys and girls saying, "I want my way"—"I"—"I," instead of telling others about the Lord Jesus.

44

How To Eat

OBJECT: Some food such as a candy bar.

LESSON: To emphasize the necessity of reading and meditating on the Bible.

PRESENTATION: Our object lesson today is about something you do at least three times a day. It's eating, of course, and I brought this candy bar as the object. I wonder if anyone can guess what the lesson is. Well, I want to remind you again of how important it is for Christians to be reading their Bibles. Some of you may be too young to read, but you can apply this lesson by asking Mother or Dad to read the Bible to you. If anyone doesn't have a Bible, I'll give you part of one afterward. But it is important for all of you to read the Word of God.

Watch me eat this candy bar. *(Eat some of it as fast as possible.)* You know, that's the way some people read their Bibles. How much do you think they get out of it? I think you see my point. If you are going to get as much as possible out of your Bible reading, you must not be in a hurry. Take time when you read God's Word.

Now watch me eat this candy. *(This time eat slowly, chewing well.)* This is not only the proper way to eat, but it is also the proper way to read God's Word. Jeremiah ate the Word of God (Jer. 15:16) and so did the Apostle John (Rev. 10:9-10), and that means taking time with your Bible so that you may understand it. Food that is gulped isn't well digested; neither does the Bible when read hurriedly mean much. Take time to think about what you read. In other words, meditate. The Bible itself stresses the importance of doing just that (Ps. 1:2; 119:97).

45

Necessary Parts

OBJECT: A watch or clock.

LESSON: Every Christian has a job to do for the Lord.

PRESENTATION: Once in a while I hear some Christian boy or girl say that he can't do anything for the Lord because he is too small. Sometimes even grownup Christians won't do anything unless they can have the biggest job or the most prominent place. I want to show you today that every Christian, no matter how small, is important to the Lord's work.

Look at this watch. Don't you imagine that the hands feel pretty important? They are always showing off to everybody! Yes, and God has to have Christians in important places. But now let me take off the back of the watch. Look at that small spring and that tiny wheel. They don't look so important, do they? And yet without those necessary parts the hands on the front wouldn't be useful. Maybe you are a spring in God's work and don't feel important. But you are important in God's program.

You know that the name on a watch means a great deal. Some manufacturers have better reputations than others. You have a name on you too if you are saved. It is that of the Lord Jesus Christ. But if you are not doing your part, then His name is disgraced. If I buy a certain make of watch and it stops in a month or so, you can be sure that I wouldn't buy the same kind again. Do you think that unsaved boys and girls will want to become Christians if they see that your Christianity doesn't work well?

Remember, will you, that no matter how small a job you may seem to have it is so important that you do it well. Then others will want to come to believe in the Lord Jesus too.

46

Unbelief

OBJECT: Choir robe or bathrobe (preferably one that is too small for you).

LESSON: Faith is vital to the life of the Christian (Heb. 12:1).

PRESENTATION: I guess you think that I'm dressed in a rather strange way today, but this is just the way some of you are dressed in your Christian lives. I'll show you what I mean.

God says that the Christian life is like a race, and every boy or girl who is a Christian is in that race. Of course, we are not supposed to lose but rather to win that race, and yet very few do. Do you know what the reason is? Do you remember the lesson about weights or hindrances in the Christian life? That is one reason why we lose the race. But there is a second reason, and that is something wrapped around us like this robe. It is unbelief. The Bible says that it wraps itself around us so that we can barely move. How fast do you think I could run dressed like this? Neither can you run the Christian life when you are all wrapped up in unbelief.

What is unbelief? It is simply not letting God have control of everything. In order to be saved you had to let Christ save you, didn't you? You couldn't do it yourself. Neither can you live the Christian life in your own strength; it has to be lived by faith (II Cor. 5:7), and that means trusting the Lord Jesus for everything. Are Dad and Mother not saved? Then trust God to save them, and ask Him in prayer about it. Ask in faith for a chance to speak to them. Ask for courage to do it, and then believe that God will give you what you have asked for. That's what faith is, and it is absolutely necessary in winning the Christian race. Don't worry about whether or not you have enough faith. Remember in whom your faith is.

47

Safe

OBJECT: An egg, a pan and a hammer.

LESSON: "Your life is hid with Christ in God" (Col. 3:3).

PRESENTATION: I am sure that some of you think that you are weak Christians, but I want to show you just how safe and secure you are. I brought along an egg to represent a Christian boy or girl. I don't suppose there is anything more delicate and fragile than an egg, so it represents well any of you who think that you are in danger of losing your salvation. Now we're going to put the egg under this frying pan and let that represent what the Bible calls being in Christ. It is simply that safe place in which God puts you when you are saved. Even though you are weak, you are perfectly safe in Christ's care and shelter. Let's just see how safe you are. Suppose the devil taps you just a little bit. *(Strike the pan with the hammer.)* Does that hurt the egg? Suppose he hits you harder. Is the egg still untouched? Suppose he pounds and pounds. Does the egg break?

Let me read the verse for today *(read Col. 3:3).* Do you see what that means? Your life is just as safe as God is. As long as God can take any blow that may come, then you will never lose your salvation. It doesn't make any difference how weak you are, for He is strong. As long as you are trusting the Lord as your Saviour, you are absolutely safe from any attack on your salvation.

But perhaps there is someone here who does not have such a secure and eternal salvation. Wouldn't you like to know that you are safe for all eternity? You can know if you will simply belive that Jesus Christ died for your sins on the cross of Calvary. Won't you tell Him just now that you want Him as your Saviour?

48

Keeping Clean

OBJECT: A wrapped cake of soap.

LESSON: To emphasize the need of cleansing for the Christian.

PRESENTATION: I'm sure all of you know what this object is used for. The soap ads we see and hear everywhere today make all kinds of wonderful claims about what this soap or that soap will do for us, but, after all, the main purpose of soap is to make us clean. I expect that most of you used some in a bath either last night or this morning before coming to church. That's a good thing to do. No one likes to be around someone who is not clean.

Soap makes us clean on the outside, but what can you do about cleaning up on the inside before coming to church? Well, there is only one way to do that and that is to confess your uncleanness or sins to the Lord and ask Him to cleanse you (I John 1:9). He has promised that if we confess our sins He will forgive us, and in that verse He is talking to Christians.

How often do you boys and girls take a bath? Once a year? Of course not—you have to bathe more often than that or you would be filthy. How do you think the inside of a Christian looks who only confesses his sins to the Lord once a year? We have to bathe often and we ought to confess our wrongs just as soon as we know that we have done something that displeased the Lord. Don't let sins accumulate but confess them right away.

Does this bar of soap do any good all wrapped up like this? No, I have to open it to use it. So, if you are going to have fellowship with the Lord, it doesn't do any good merely to listen to what I have said. You have to use it, and if there is something you ought to confess to the Lord, then why not do it right now? You'll enjoy the rest of the day much more.

49

Ticklish?

OBJECT: Yourself or another person.

LESSON: To emphasize the need for being sensitive to the truth of God.

PRESENTATION: Will someone come and help me this morning with the object lesson? All right, I want you to try to find out where I am ticklish. Go ahead. Tickle me in several places. You see, I'm quite ticklish in some places and not at all in others. Do you know why that is? In some places the skin is very thin and I am sensitive while in others it is thick and calloused. For instance, on the ball of your foot hardly anyone is ticklish, but just an inch away, under the arch, almost everyone is.

Boys and girls, I hope this little experiment will teach you a very important lesson. The Lord wants us to be very sensitive to all that He says in His Word, and—may I put it this way— He wants us to jump when He speaks. Some Christians aren't this way at all, for their hearts become just like the thick-skinned parts of the body and are not sensitive to sin. The Bible warns Christians against this condition when it says, "Harden not your hearts" (Heb. 3:8). That word "harden" means calloused, so God is saying in this verse, "Don't let your heart become covered with callouses." God wants us to be sensitive to sin, just as sensitive as a ticklish person is ticklish. When you do something wrong God expects you to feel it right away and not to ignore the fact that you have displeased Him. Also God wants you to be sensitive to His leading day by day.

Would you like to know the name of a good heart medicine to keep your heart tender? It's God's Word, the Bible. Reading, knowing, loving and obeying this Book will keep you sensitive to God's will. "Thy word have I hid in mine heart, that I might not sin against thee" (Ps. 119:11).

50

The Earnest

OBJECT: The teacher should have some money with which to buy something from one of the pupils.

LESSON: To teach the truths concerning the earnest of the spirit (Eph. 1:14).

PRESENTATION: I noticed the other day, John, that you had a nice looking wallet. Would you come up here and show it to everyone? How would you like to sell it to me? You will, good. How much do you want for it? All right, I'll buy it, only I don't have the full price with me today. Would you take a dollar from me now and hold the wallet for me until next Sunday when I'll pay you the rest of the money?

Boys and girls, this dollar that I just gave John is called earnest money. It simply signifies that I am in earnest about buying the wallet and that John is in earnest about selling it. It guarantees that the deal will go through because neither party can back out once earnest money has been given and received. Did you know that God has given each Christian an earnest of salvation? God's earnest isn't money; it's the Holy Spirit. And His presence in your heart is the guarantee that God will some day take you to heaven.

I want you to remember two things about the earnest. The first is this: just as I am going to come back next Sunday and get possession of my wallet, so the Lord Jesus is coming back to get us and take us to heaven to be with Him forever. The fact that the Holy Spirit lives in your heart is the guarantee that Jesus will do this. The second thing is this: while we are waiting for the Lord we must be careful to live lives that are pleasing to the Holy Spirit. Every Christian belongs to Christ, and the Lord wants us to be very careful how we live every day until He comes back to get us. The Holy Spirit, the earnest, will remind you of this.

51

Believing in the Resurrection

OBJECT: A bandage made by wrapping a finger or hand in newspaper and then taping it so that the whole thing will slip off easily.

LESSON: To illustrate what John saw when he looked into Christ's tomb the first Easter (John 20:8).

PRESENTATION: You remember that the Bible says that when Peter and John went to Christ's tomb that first Easter, one look was enough to convince them that the Lord was risen. I want to show you why that look was so convincing. If I were to wrap my finger in adhesive tape and then wanted to take the tape off, what would I have to do? Of course, I would have to unwrap it because it wouldn't slip off. When a person died in Bible times they wrapped the entire body in strips of cloth, just like I wrapped this other finger, and the Lord's body was wrapped that way after the crucifixion. If anyone had stolen Christ's body from the tomb (as some unbelievers say) they wouldn't have taken time to unwrap it but would have stolen it wrappings and all. But when John looked into that tomb he saw the wrappings and knew instantly that the Lord's body had not merely been stolen.

He did not just see the wrappings lying in a heap, however. They were there just as if they were still wrapped around the body. It was like this (hold up the prepared bandage which will be shaped like your finger or hand). Yards and yards of cloth were not strung out all over the tomb.

Christ is alive, but let me ask you how you know it is true. John saw and believed. The Bible tells us it is true. But the best way you can know that Jesus lives is by receiving Him into your heart right now if you have never done that. If you are a Christian you know He is alive because you walk and talk with Him. John saw and believed. Do you?

52

String

OBJECT: A piece of heavy and a piece of light string.

LESSON: To show the increased strength of a united testimony.

PRESENTATION: Boys and girls, today I want to show you one of the reasons why it is important for you to come regularly to our meetings. Why do we come, anyway? One reason is this: to bring other boys and girls to know the Lord Jesus Christ as their own Saviour. Why is it important for all of us to come?

Our group is like this piece of string. It is one group, yet it is made up of many individuals, just as this one piece of string is made up of many little strands. I want one of you to try to break this piece of string in two. It's rather hard to do, isn't it? Try this smaller piece. That breaks much more easily, doesn't it? What makes the difference? The smaller piece does not have so many strands in it as the other has.

Do you see the application? The writer of the book of Hebrews warns us against forsaking the assembling of ourselves together (10:25), that is, not coming together to these meetings. If many of us come, we have a strong testimony. If only a few come, our testimony is weaker. And if there are only a few, then Satan may be able to stop our meetings altogether.

Let's remember to come regularly and to bring others with us, so that our testimony for the Lord will be strong. If there is anyone here today who is not saved but would like to be, just tell the Lord Jesus, who died for you, and He will come into your heart.

53

Yourself

OBJECT: Yourself.

LESSON: To show that honor is bestowed on weak members of
the body of Christ (I Cor. 12:22-25).

PRESENTATION: Some of you Christians may have the idea that
you're not of much use to the Lord, perhaps because of age or
weakness. That's not true. Consider, for instance, this little
finger of mine. It's very weak and it doesn't look very useful,
but without it there are lots of things I couldn't do. Maybe you
are only a little finger but God needs your life.

"Well," you say, "I don't have any abilities—I can't attract
anyone to the Lord Jesus." Look at my foot, for instance. I
can't play the piano or draw beautiful pictures with it, but
without my foot I'd have a hard time getting around. And,
furthermore, I think so much of my feet that I buy socks and
shoes to put on them. God also gives honor to those members
of the body of Christ which seem to have less honor. Maybe
you're only a foot, but God needs you to do things for Him, and
He will honor you for it.

If you happen to have a great deal of ability, then God doesn't
need to bestow honor on you. God tells us that He has done
this in order that there may be no divisions in the body of
Christ, in other words, so that you who have more gifts than
others will not look down on those who have fewer gifts.

Don't ever think, then, that you're too insignificant to be used
of the Lord. He needs little fingers and feet, yes, and arms and
faces—all to be used to His glory. Even if you're only a little
finger, if you let the Lord control and use you, He will bestow
abundant honor on you and reward you for it.

54

One Body

OBJECT: A newspaper.

LESSON: "But now are they many members, yet but one body" (I Cor. 12:20).

PRESENTATION: Paul the apostle tells us that the church—that is, all Christians, not any certain denomination—is the body of Christ. There is one body, he says, but many members, and each saved person, even boys and girls, are members of that body, and each has something different to do.

Let's look through this newspaper to illustrate this: Here is a story about the President, and Christ also has public officials in His body. All of them should be serving the Lord in whatever public office they have. Here's the sports page, and the Lord Jesus also has athletes in His body. Here's the financial section, and God also has businessmen who are living for Him. He wants men to earn money, but not for themselves. There have been faithful businessmen who have been used of God to support many missionaries, and the Lord has blessed them for it. Here are the advertisements, and every Christian ought to be a good advertisement for the Lord Jesus Christ. The Lord may choose to use you as a full-page ad, or perhaps only as a small want ad. Maybe He will want you to advertise Him in the sports world, or in the business world, or in the ministry, or on the mission field, but wherever you are, do your very best for Him.

It takes all these kinds of people to make up the body of Christ, just as it takes all these various parts to make up this paper. I can't tell what part you have to play but, whatever it is, remember that if you are saved you are a member of the body of Christ.

55

The Believer's Works

OBJECT: A silver coin and several matches.

LESSON: To show the different kinds of works done by the believer (I Cor. 3:11-15).

PRESENTATION: We know that no one is saved by works (Eph. 2:9), but only by faith in the Lord Jesus Christ. After Christians are saved, however, works have an important part in their lives. Throughout our Christian lives we are building on Christ, as the foundation, one of two kinds of works—those that will remain or those that will not. When the Lord comes, He is going to judge every Christian according to the works he has done since he was saved. I want to show you what is going to happen at that judgment.

Here comes a believer who hasn't built well. His works are wood, hay or stubble, and when the fire of God's judgment tries them, here's what happens. (*Light one of the matches.*) All his works burn because they weren't good works, although he himself is saved. Here comes another believer. His works are of gold, silver and precious stones, and this is what happens when they are judged. (*Light a match under the coin.*) His works abide, and the Lord says that he will receive a reward.

The question for your heart today is: What kind of works am I building? Will they abide or will they be burned? Let's be careful, as Christians, to build works of gold, silver and precious stones. If you are not a Christian, all the works in the world won't help you. You need a foundation to build on, and that foundation is Jesus Christ. The way to have Him is to receive Him by faith as your Saviour.

56

Want Ads

OBJECT: A page of want ads from any newspaper.

LESSON: Witnessing for Christ.

PRESENTATION: I suppose that most of you boys and girls skip these pages in the paper, but when you get a little older you'll read them as many people do. But there's an object lesson for us in these want ads, because every Christian is, in a sense, a want ad. We Christians are advertising a Person, the Lord Jesus Christ, our Saviour.

Let's look at some of these want ads. Here is one for a house. You notice that it tells how beautiful the house is, how large it is, what good condition it is in, and all the advantages of it. The Lord Jesus Christ, the Person we are advertising, is much more beautiful than any house. And yet, so often Christians make it seem as if being a Christian were the worst thing in the world.

You notice, too, that although want ads are very small they are very important and many, many people use them. In the same way, you may think that you cannot do much for the Lord, but never forget that unsaved people are always looking to you to see if this Christianity of yours is a good thing or not. You may never be a great preacher or teacher, but you can and should be a good witness and win others to Christ though you are only want-ad size.

Have you ever noticed that many of these ads mention a selling price? Of course, if you want to buy any of these articles, you have to pay for them. But that is not true of us as Christian want ads, because we advertise something that is absolutely free. To have Jesus Christ is to have salvation, and God wants to give that to you as a free gift. If any of you have never received this gift, you may do so today by simply opening your hearts and accepting by faith the Lord Jesus Christ as your very own Saviour from sin. Then, when you are saved, be a good want ad for your Saviour.

57

A Bad Light Bulb

OBJECT: A light bulb that has burned out.

LESSON: To show that a little sin may ruin a Christian's testimony.

PRESENTATION: This light bulb looks all right, doesn't it? But there's just one thing wrong with it—it doesn't work. It has burned out. (*If an electric outlet is available, show that the bulb is burned out.*) Today we are going to show how this bulb is like many Christians who have no testimony for the Lord. They are like this bulb—they're not shining for the Lord.

This bulb—although I'm not certain—may have been exposed to the wind and the rain, and yet that didn't cause it to go out. Some of you are too young to have been tested a great deal, but many Christians have to suffer much for the Lord, and yet He brings them through with a brighter testimony for Himself.

Do you know why this bulb burned out? Let me show you. (*If possible, break the glass from around the stem.*) Look at this wire. You see, it's broken, and that's why the bulb won't light. That's just what happens to many Christians. They can withstand many temptations, but some little sin can ruin their testimony for the Lord.

How about you today? Are there little things in your life which are ruining your testimony for the Lord Jesus? When you're out playing, do you fight with other children? Do you do what Mother asks you to do? Are you telling other boys and girls about the Lord Jesus? It may be just a little thing in your sight—it's big in God's sight—but just as it took only a little break in this wire to put the light out, so it may take only one of these sins to put out your testimony for the Lord Jesus Christ.

58

A Good Light Bulb

OBJECT: An ordinary light bulb that is attached, or the bulb in a flashlight.

LESSON: Abiding in Christ is necessary for fruitfulness (John 15:5).

PRESENTATION: Boys and girls, do you think this is a good bulb? You can't tell unless I screw it in, can you? (*Screw it in so that it lights.*) Now do you think it's good? You know it is. This bulb unattached is like many Christian boys and girls. They are saved but they don't give light for the Lord Jesus. When they look like this (*bulb not lit*) you can't tell if they are Christians or not. But when they are like this (*bulb lit*), you know for certain that they are.

What makes the difference? It's simply this: the bulb doesn't light unless it has contact with the source of power. Our Lord Jesus said, "For without me ye can do nothing" (John 15:5*b*). This means that unless you are in fellowship with Him every moment of the day you can't shine for Him. Do you know what breaks our fellowship with Him? Sin. If there is sin in the lives of any of you Christian boys and girls today, confess it right now and get back into fellowship with the Lord Jesus so that you may shine for Him.

How does your Christian life look today? Like this (*bulb unscrewed*)? Or like this (*bulb lit*)?

59

A Broken Fingernail

OBJECT: A broken fingernail.

LESSON: To show that fellowship with Christ is necessary to be a testimony for Christ.

PRESENTATION: Look at my fingernail, boys and girls. What's the matter with it? Yes, it's broken. I hit it the other day and was going to cut it off when I realized it would help me teach an object lesson.

When the Lord Jesus was here on earth He said that without Him we Christians could do nothing (John 15:5). Since God has left us here on earth to do things for Him and to be a testimony for our Saviour, it is absolutely necessary that we be able to do those things all the time. But we will never be able to have a strong testimony for the Lord unless we are in constant fellowship with Him. This fingernail is no good to me the way it is, and it certainly does not look very nice; it's just like a boy or girl whose fellowship with Christ is broken because he or she is of no use to the Lord.

What do you think I'm going to have to do with this fingernail? Certainly, I'll have to cut it off, and that's exactly what happens to the testimony of a Christian who is not in fellowship with Christ. The Lord Jesus said, "If any man abide not in me, he is cast forth as a branch, and is withered" (John 15:6).

How does your testimony look? Is it like this? (*Show an unbroken fingernail.*) Or is it like this? (*Show the broken fingernail.*) If it's like that, then you had better get back into fellowship by telling the Lord that you've sinned, and then keep in fellowship by constantly reading your Bible, and by praying. Will you do this right now as we pray silently? Don't be a broken-fingernail Christian.

60

Hair

OBJECT: Head of hair.

LESSON: To show God's care for His own (Matt. 10:30).

PRESENTATION: How many hairs do you think are on your head? Well, if you have red hair, you have about 90,000. If you have black hair, there are about 103,000. On the other hand, if you have brown hair, there are more than 109,000 hairs on your head, but if you are a blond, you probably have 140,000 hairs.

Each of you has many, many hairs on your head, and I'm sure that if you started to count them you would tire very quickly. But do you know that God knows how many hairs are on your head? Listen to this verse: "But the very hairs of your head are all numbered" (Matt. 10:30).

This verse shows us the loving care of God, who numbered all the hairs of our heads. If God knows how many hairs are on your head, don't you think He also knows every detail in your life? There's no problem in your life that He cannot solve, and there's no need that He cannot meet. If He knows the number of hairs on your head, He certainly knows when you need strength to overcome temptation, or when you need help in telling someone else about the Lord Jesus.

Remember this little lesson, boys and girls. Every time you comb your hair, for instance, remember just how much your heavenly Father cares for you. But also remember that this is true only if you have believed in the Lord Jesus. So if you have never trusted Christ, do that right now.